The Male-to-Female Dictionary

The Male-to-Female Dictionary

The Handy Guide to the
Babble of the Sexes

SUSAN SHAPIRO

ILLUSTRATIONS BY CAROL LAY

A Byron Preiss Visual Publications, Inc. Book

BOULEVARD BOOKS • NEW YORK

THE MALE-TO-FEMALE DICTIONARY

A Boulevard Book/published by arrangement with
Byron Preiss Visual Publications, Inc.

PRINTING HISTORY
Boulevard trade paperback edition/August 1996

Art by Carol Lay
Cover design by Don Welsh
Interior design by Jessica Shatan
Executive Editor: Michael Sagalyn
Editor: Dinah Dunn

The Putnam Berkley World Wide Web site address is
http://www.berkley.com

ISBN: 1-57297-116-9

BOULEVARD
Boulevard Books are published by The Berkley Publishing Group,
200 Madison Avenue, New York, New York 10016.
BOULEVARD and its logo are trademarks
belonging to Berkley Publishing Corporation.

PRINTED IN THE UNITED STATES OF AMERICA

10   9   8   7   6   5   4   3   2   1

Contents

Introduction

Venturing into foreign territory is often stressful and intimidating. Yet by learning the language, laws, and weird rituals of the locals, you can overcome communication barriers, thrive in an alien environment, and avoid danger.

Whether you are planning a brief visit or a long and twisted journey, it can't hurt to learn the rules of the road from a seasoned and cynical traveler—one who has seen the sights, taken wild and ridiculous risks, and survived.

Here are travel tips, conversion charts, and translations for all the exotic and erotic situations tourists are likely to encounter. We're sure the *Male-to-Female Dictionary* will prove to be an invaluable companion.

So relax, buckle your seat belt in case of turbulence, and get ready for the trip of your life . . .

GRAMMAR

Female	Male
PRONOUNS:	
"We"	"I"
POSSESSIVE ADJECTIVES:	
"Our"	"My"
POSSESSIVE PRONOUNS:	
"Ours"	"Mine"
IRREGULAR VERBS:	
Marrying, Committing, Procreating	Waiting, Hesitating, Procrastinating
REFLEXIVE PRONOUNS:	
"Ourselves"	"Myself"
TENSES:	
Future, as in "Where is this relationship going?" and *Past*, as in "You said we'd spend our lives together."	*Present*, as in "Let's go to bed," and *Past*, as in "We used to have fun together before you started in about where this relationship is going."
NOUN FORMS:	
To make plural, add ring	Stay singular as long as possible
ARTICLES:	
Cosmo's "How Faithful Is Your Man?" survey	*Penthouse* centerfold

TYPES OF WOMEN AND MEN:
Different Regions and Dialects

Don't assume that all natives you encounter are the same. Geographic and genetic variations often determine differences in dress code, dialogue, dating rituals, and daily demeanor.

Type (Female)	Field Guide Translations
Baby Doll	"Take care of me"
Gold Digger	"You and your credit card should take care of me"
Career Woman	"I can take care of myself"
Feminist	"Womankind can take care of itself"
Sex Bomb	"I'll really take care of you, baby"
Glamour Goddess	"Take care of me in the manner to which I'm accustomed—when I'm done putting on my makeup"
Space Cadet	"Someone take care of me, please"
Victim	"Nobody ever takes care of me"
Artist	"My creations are my babies"
Bleeding Heart	"I'll take care of all the starving children"
Mommy	"I'll take good care of you and the kids"
Earth Mother	"I'll take care of everybody"

TYPES OF WOMEN AND MEN:
Different Regions and Dialects

Type (Male)	Field Guide Translations
Frat Boy	"Take care of me tonight"
Marrying Man	"I'll take care of you forever"
Stud	"I'll really take care of you, baby"
Blue-Collar Boy	"I'll take care of you—and your car"
Boy Scout	"I'll take care of you, on my honor"
Power Player	"I'll take care of you in the manner to which you're accustomed—when I'm done taking care of business"
Artist	"My brilliant, important creations justify my lousy, self-involved life"
Victimizer	"I'll take care of you but good"
Politico	"I need power to take care of all the starving children"
Daddy	"I'll take care of you and the kids"
Sugar Daddy	"Me and my credit card will take care of you"
Godfather	"I'll take care of everybody"

COMMON EXPRESSIONS

The following are fundamental phrases you'll hear over and over. We suggest that you become very familiar with these phrases. Inflection varies accordingly.

COMMON PHRASES: FEMALE

"Where's this relationship going?"

"Where's the ring?"

"It's that time of the month."

"Where are we going for dinner?"

"Why can't you clean up after yourself?"

"I need security."

COMMON PHRASES: MALE

"Let's go to bed."

"Where's the remote?"

"What's the matter? You on the rag?"

"What's for dinner?"

"Why can't you leave my stuff where I put it?"

"I need space."

WHAT TO SAY AND DO

When socializing with people from another culture, you must understand customary greetings and expressions of courtesy and respect. To make it clear you're an ally, try the following:

WHAT TO SAY TO A WOMAN . . .

"You look great, have you lost weight?"

"That's a pretty dress."

"You're beautiful."

"You have perfect breasts."

"You have a perfect body."

"You have a better body than all my past girlfriends."

WHAT TO SAY TO A MAN . . .

"Your arms look big, do you work out?"

"That's a handsome suit."

"You look handsome."

"You're huge."

"I can't believe how big you are."

"You're bigger than all my past boyfriends."

WHAT TO DO FOR A WOMAN . . .

Bring her flowers

Bring her perfume

Take her out to dinner

Be happy to see her when she comes home from work

Call if you're going to be late

Hug her

Cuddle after sex

Call if you're going to be late

WHAT TO DO FOR A WOMAN . . .

Display affection in public

Put her picture up

When going out, ask if you can pick up anything for her at the store

Talk about where your relationship is going

Ask questions about her

Listen to her when she talks

Call if you're going to be late

WHAT TO DO FOR A MAN . . .

Keep a six-pack of his favorite beer in the fridge

Cook his favorite dinner

Watch the ball game with him

Be happy to see him when he comes home from work

Thank him for calling when he's going to be late

Say, "It's not your fault," when something screws up

Let him emotionally withdraw

WHAT TO DO FOR A MAN . . .

Display affection in public

Put his picture up

When going out, ask if you can pick up anything for him at the store

Don't ask where the relationship is going

Listen to him

WHAT NEVER TO DO TO A WOMAN . . .

Explain why she's silly to be upset

Ogle other women when you're with her

Say you'll do something, then forget to do it

Show up late without calling

Give her ten minutes to get ready

Emotionally withdraw when she's talking about her feelings

WHAT NEVER TO DO TO A WOMAN . . .

Read the newspaper while she's talking to you about her feelings

Turn on the TV while she's talking to you about her feelings

Offer solutions when she's talking about her feelings

Ignore her

Say "Nothing," and shrug when she asks, "What's wrong?"

Put your work before her

Put your friends before her

WHAT NEVER TO DO TO A MAN . . .

Offer unsolicited advice on how he should change

Try to control his behavior

Ogle other men when you're with him

Nag him for forgetting to do something

Yell at him for being late

Yell at him for giving you ten minutes to get ready

Criticize what he hasn't done

Criticize him for emotionally withdrawing when you're talking about your feelings

WHAT NEVER TO DO TO A MAN . . .

Criticize him in front of his friends

Criticize him in front of his family

Criticize him in public

Criticize him in private

Say "Nothing," and shrug when he asks, "What's wrong?"

Put your work before him

Put your friends before him

You must also be aware of taboos. You don't want to unwittingly offend. Avoid the following at all costs:

WHAT NEVER TO SAY TO A WOMAN . . .

"You gained some weight, you look great."

"That's a handsome suit."

"You gained some weight, are you pregnant?"

"Have you ever thought about breast implants?"

"Are those real?"

"I like a lady with a big appetite."

WHAT NEVER TO SAY TO A WOMAN . . .

"You're so needy."

"Don't be upset."

"What's the matter? You on the rag?"

"Did you come?"

"My old girlfriend had a great body."

"My old girlfriend had multiple orgasms every time."

"You're just like your mother."

WHAT NEVER TO SAY TO A MAN . . .

"You look cute."

"But my mother's birthday dinner is more important than the Super Bowl."

"Marry me or else."

"I hope you don't mind I threw out those old sneakers."

"I think you've had a few too many."

"I told you so."

WHAT NEVER TO SAY TO A MAN . . .

"Have you ever thought of a penile implant?"

"Receding hairline, huh?"

"Let's talk about where our relationship is going."

"I didn't come."

"My old boyfriend was a great lover."

"My old boyfriend could do it five times a night."

"You're just like your father."

PACKING

To make sure you're well equipt for your journey, there are certain things to always keep handy.

WHAT A WOMAN PACKS:

Umbrella

Map

Chapstick

Checkbook

Calorie counter

WHAT A MAN PACKS:

Big key rings

Rolling papers

Swiss Army knife

Lots of cash

Condoms

TRANSLATIONS

Don't let language barriers confuse or confound you. Here's a guide to translating common lingo into literal meaning.

FIX-UPS: FEMALE-TO-ENGLISH

Female . . .	English . . .
"Is he nice?"	"And not a commitment-phobe like my last boyfriend?"
"What does he do?"	"Is he buying dinner?"
"Has he ever been married?"	"Has he made at least one real commitment in his lifetime?"
"Has he been in therapy?"	"Will he be able to make at least one real commitment in his lifetime?"
"How tall is he?"	"Can I wear heels?"
"Where does he live?"	"Does he have room for me?"
"What does he look like?"	"What does he look like?"

FIX-UPS: MALE-TO-ENGLISH

Male . . .

"Is she nice?"

"How do you know her?"

"You think I'd like her?"

"What does she do?"

"You think she'll like me?"

"How tall is she?"

"Where does she live?"

English . . .

"What does she look like?"

"If she's so cute, why aren't you going out with her?"

"What does she look like?"

"What does she look like?"

"You think she'll sleep with me?"

"What does her body look like?"

"Is she good-looking enough to overcome being geographically undesirable?"

FIX-UP FOLLOW-UP: FEMALE-TO-ENGLISH

Female . . .

"He came over right on time, at 8:00, wearing nice black jeans and a beige shirt and matching blazer . . . He was cute, 5-foot-9½, not quite tall enough, but he drove a brown BMW and took me to a nice Italian restaurant. He said he was thinking of leaving his big law firm for a smaller practice . . . He ordered for me; he's a Leo, kind of controlling and not really compatible with my moon sign, but he treated for dinner, and opened the door for me. He went out with his last girlfriend, a legal secretary, for two years. He said she was crazy but I think he has a commitment problem. It was a nice conversation, even though he talked about himself most of the time, but he was a good kisser and said he'd call tomorrow, so maybe . . ."

English . . .

"I liked him."

FIX-UP FOLLOW-UP: MALE-TO-ENGLISH

Male . . .

"She was cute."

English . . .

"I liked her."

AT THE BAR: FEMALE-TO-ENGLISH

Female . . .

English . . .

"I've never been here before."

"I've never seen you here before."

"Do you come here often?"

"Are you a drunk?"

"Thanks, I'd love a drink."

"Don't even think about getting me drunk and inviting me to your place."

"Thanks, my girlfriend would love a drink too."

"Don't even think about getting us drunk and inviting us to your place."

"Here's my card."

"Call me."

"Are you listed?"

"Give me your phone number."

"I'll call you."

"I'll call you."

AT THE BAR: MALE-TO-ENGLISH

Male . . .	English . . .
"Do you come here often?"	"Are you a lush?"
"Can I buy you a drink?"	"Can I take you home?"
"Can I buy your girlfriend a drink?"	"Can I take both of you home?"
"My wife and I are separated."	"She's home and I'm out bar-hopping."
"My wife doesn't understand me."	"My wife doesn't understand why I pick up girls in bars."
"Are you listed?"	"Give me your phone number."
"I'll call you."	"I won't call you."

FIRST DATES: FEMALE-TO-ENGLISH

Female . . .	English . . .
"Do you want to have lunch?"	"I'm not sure I'm attracted to you."
"Okay, I'd love to meet you for a drink."	"What's wrong? I'm not good enough to buy dinner for?"
"So, do you live alone?"	"Are you married, gay, living with someone or otherwise unavailable? Tell me now."
"Have you ever been married?"	"Or have you been a complete commitment-phobe your whole life?"
"Do you have any children?"	"Can you support children?"
"I think it's dumb to get married young these days."	"You're not so young anymore; what are you waiting for?"
"I'm not looking for anything serious right now."	"I'm looking for something serious right now."

FIRST DATES: FEMALE-TO-ENGLISH

Female . . .

"My last boyfriend was too young."

"So why is a handsome man like you still single?"

"Have you had many serious relationships?"

"I tend to be monogamous."

"I'd love to see you again."

"I think honesty is essential in a relationship."

English . . .

"My last boyfriend couldn't commit to a one-night stand."

"So what's wrong with you? Tell me now."

"Are you infected with anything?"

"Do you screw around a lot? Tell me now."

"I'm very attracted to you."

"Are you a sociopath? Tell me now."

FIRST DATES: MALE-TO-ENGLISH

Male . . .	English . . .
"Do you want to have lunch?"	"I'm not sure I'm attracted to you."
"Okay, let's have a drink."	"I'm not sure I'm attracted enough to buy you dinner."
"So, do you live alone?"	"Are you sleeping with anyone now?"
"Have you ever been married?"	"Are you desperate to be married by your next birthday?"
"Do you have any kids?"	"Are you one of those women who expects a man to support you and your kids?"
"I think it's dumb to get married young these days."	"I think it's dumb to get married these days."
"I'm not looking for anything serious right now."	"I'm not looking for anything serious right now."

FIRST DATES: MALE-TO-ENGLISH

Male . . .	English . . .
"My last girlfriend was crazy."	"My last girlfriend dumped me."
"Have you had many serious relationships?"	"Are you infected with anything?"
"So why is a beautiful woman like you still single?"	"Are you sleeping with anyone now?"
"I tend to be monogamous."	"Are you sleeping with anyone now?"
"I'd love to see you again."	"I'm attracted to you."
"How about a nightcap?"	"How about sleeping over tonight?"
"I think honesty is essential in a relationship."	"Are you sleeping with anyone now?"

AT THE RESTAURANT: FEMALE-TO-ENGLISH

Female . . .	English . . .
"Mexican isn't my favorite."	"I hope you're not thinking of taking me to Benny's Burritos."
"I'm not in the mood for a hamburger."	"Don't even think about Burger King."
"I'll have a salad and diet soda."	"I hate my thighs."
"What are you having?"	"How much do you want to spend?"
"I never eat fried foods."	"You're not really going to put that tub of grease into your body, are you?"
"I'm happy with mine, thanks."	"I'm territorial about food, and if you put your fingers in mine, it's over."
"No more wine, thanks."	"Don't even think about getting me drunk and inviting me to your place."

AT THE RESTAURANT: FEMALE-TO-ENGLISH

Female . . .

English . . .

"I never eat dessert."

"You're not really going to put that tub of chocolate into your body, are you?"

"Okay, but just a taste."

"You'd better order something else, 'cause I'm finishing this tub of chocolate."

"I'm going to powder my nose."

"You pay the check."

"Can I leave a tip?"

"You're not leaving enough tip, cheapskate."

"Shall we split the check?"

"You pay the check."

"Next time's on me."

"I want to see you again."

"I'm cooking you dinner next time."

"I want to see you again without clothes on."

AT THE RESTAURANT: MALE-TO-ENGLISH

Male . . .	English . . .
"I don't like Mexican either."	"Guess we're not going to Benny's Burritos."
"Yeah, I'm trying to cut down on meat too."	"Guess we're not going to Burger King."
"Order anything you want."	"Within reason."
"Is that all you're having?"	"Oh no, are you one of those salad-nibblers who'll make me feel like a pig?"
"Yeah, sure, have the lobster."	"I hope my credit card goes through."
"Let's see the wine list."	"I'm just trying to impress you. I'd rather see the beer list."

AT THE RESTAURANT: MALE-TO-ENGLISH

Male . . .

"Yours looks great."

"If you don't like it, send it back."

"Have some more wine."

"It's on me."

"I think men should always treat."

"I'm cooking you dinner next time."

English . . .

"I think sharing food is romantic."

"Are you always so high-maintenance?"

"Let's get drunk and go to my place."

"I want to see you again."

"I want to see you again without clothes on."

"I want to marry you."

AT THE MOVIES: FEMALE-TO-ENGLISH

Female . . .

"Let's see the new Meg Ryan movie."

"I'll get the refreshments."

"She's kind of phony-looking, don't you think?"

"*Dumb and Dumber* wouldn't be my first choice."

"It's cold in here."

"That preview was great."

"Do you like foreign movies?"

"I think Woody Allen's a jerk, don't you?"

English . . .

"Let's see something romantic and hold hands."

"I want my own popcorn."

"Stop ogling Melanie Griffith's breasts."

"You're not really going to pay money to watch fart jokes, are you?"

"Put your arm around me."

"Ask me to see it with you."

"Can you read?"

"If you ever sleep with my daughter, you're a dead man."

AT THE MOVIES: MALE-TO-ENGLISH

Male . . .	English . . .
"Sure, let's go see the new Meg Ryan movie."	"I'd rather see *Dumb and Dumber*."
"I'll get the refreshments."	"I want my own popcorn, Milk Duds, and Hershey bar."
"He's kind of dumb, don't you think?"	"Stop ogling Brad Pitt's biceps."
"I like some foreign movies."	"I like foreign movies with naked foreign women in them."
"Yeah, they are really cute together."	"I'd rather be watching Bruce Willis blow people up."
"Are you cold?"	"Want to make out?"
"That preview was great, don't you think?"	"Play your cards right and I'll ask you to see it with me."
"I still think Woody Allen's movies are funny."	"I'll stay away from your daughter if you don't adopt twelve kids and ten pets."

IN THE CAR: FEMALE-TO-ENGLISH

Female . . .	English . . .
"We need gas."	"Why drive with half a tank when we can drive with a full tank?"
"Let's look at the map."	". . . before we waste two hours driving around lost like idiots . . ."
"Let's ask for directions."	". . . before we waste six hours driving around lost like idiots . . ."
"Can we turn the radio down a bit?"	"Are you trying to avoid talking about our relationship again?"
"Aren't you going a bit fast, honey?"	"Do we really have to drag-race the redneck psycho in the black van who just cut us off?"
"I need a rest stop."	"I need to freshen up, brush my hair, reapply my makeup, check my phone messages, stop in the 7-Eleven next door for tampons and deodorant, and buy a few T-shirts at the cute little souvenir shop . . ."

IN THE CAR: MALE-TO-ENGLISH

Male . . .	English . . .
"Do you mind if I drive?"	"I'm driving."
"We're fine on gas."	"This car can get eighty miles on empty, watch."
"It's around here somewhere."	"I would rather drive around lost for two hours than ask for directions."
"No, that's okay, we'll find it."	"I would rather drive around lost for six hours than look at the map."
"Thanks for your help, honey."	"I'm driving."
"Just a bit over the speed limit."	"I'm driving."
"I need a rest stop."	"I need to pull over on the side of the road to take a leak."

HOUSEHOLD REPAIRS: FEMALE-TO-ENGLISH

Female . . .

"Let's call the repairman."

"But you've been at it for three and a half hours."

"I'll pay for the repairman . . ."

English . . .

". . . before you break it even worse, like last time."

"Let's call the repairman before it's completely ruined."

"Just to avoid cleaning up the mess you're making."

HOUSEHOLD REPAIRS: MALE-TO-ENGLISH

Male . . .

"Why pay a repairman?"

"Just one more turn and I'll . . ."

"You know, the workmanship is pretty shoddy on this . . ."

English . . .

". . . when I can fix it in no time for free?"

". . . break it worse than before, like last time . . ."

"Let's call the repairman."

IN THE BEDROOM: FEMALE-TO-ENGLISH

Female . . .

"Let's turn the lights out."

"I've never done this before."

"I'm on a diet."

"Do you have something?"

"I might have something here."

"That feels nice."

"I love you."

"Call me."

English . . .

"I'm self-conscious about my body."

"I've never done this with you before."

"Tell me I have a beautiful body."

"Don't even try to get out of wearing a condom."

"Condoms are in the second drawer to the right. Lubricated or latex?"

"So keep doing it for more than thirty seconds."

"I love you forever."

"Call me tomorrow or I'll fly into a paranoid panic."

IN THE BEDROOM: MALE-TO-ENGLISH

Male . . .	English . . .
"Let's keep the lights on."	"I want to see your body."
"It's been a long time."	"It's been two weeks."
"I've been working out a lot."	"Tell me I have bigger muscles than your last boyfriend."
"I didn't bring anything."	"You're not going to make me wear a condom, are you?"
"Does that feel good?"	"Hello? Are you alive?"
"I love you."	"I love sleeping with you."
"I'll call you."	"I'll call you next week, when you're no longer speaking to me."

GIFTS: FEMALE-TO-ENGLISH

Female . . .

"What a lovely scarf. Where did you get it?"

"Tulips! How sweet!"

"One rose—how romantic!"

"A Springsteen CD—how imaginative!"

"Edible underwear! How sexy!"

"Wow! Great! A Knicks T-shirt!"

"Black lingerie! How pretty!"

English . . .

"Can it be returned?"

"Why not roses?"

"You couldn't spring for the other eleven?"

"A Springsteen CD—how impersonal!"

"Edible underwear! How perverted!"

"Wow! Great! My kid brother will love it!"

"Oh good, a present for yourself."

GIFTS: MALE-TO-ENGLISH

Male . . .	English . . .
"What a great purple sweater. Where did you get it?"	"I'd rather die than be seen in a purple sweater."
"Oh great! Opera tickets."	"Oh good, a present for yourself."
"Thanks for the cologne."	"I'd rather die than smell like flowers in public."
"A homemade book with poetry, my high school picture, and ticket stubs to movies we've seen together—how creative!"	"A homemade book with poetry, my high school picture, and ticket stubs to movies we've seen together—how obsessive!"
"Honey, what a great tie."	"I'd rather have a Springsteen CD."
"A book on relationships! Thanks!"	"So now we can spend ten more hours talking about our relationship instead of having one."

FRIENDS: FEMALE-TO-ENGLISH

Female . . .

"I really like Steve and Sheryl."

"Let's have dinner with Steve and Sheryl."

"My friend Pam's just being protective."

"So, what did you and your buddy Howie study in college?"

"So, how close are you and Howie?"

English . . .

"I really like that you have one friend who is happily married."

"Maybe they'll rub off on you."

"My friend Pam thinks I should dump you."

". . . drinking and screwing girls?"

"Get rid of him."

FRIENDS: MALE-TO-ENGLISH

Male . . .	English . . .
"Your friend Pam is a real live wire."	"Your friend Pam is a real slut."
"We had an interesting conversation."	"She wouldn't shut up."
"I don't want to have dinner with Steve and Sheryl."	". . . so we can hear about how wonderful marriage is for ten hours."
"Howie's my only friend who understands me."	"Howie's my only friend who's single and can go barhopping with me."
"Okay, we'll invite Steve and Sheryl over for dinner."	"I'd rather go out and get drunk with Howie."

DEPRESSION: FEMALE-TO-ENGLISH

Female . . .	English . . .
"Nothing's wrong."	"Something's wrong."
"It's not about you."	"It's about you."
"There's nothing you can do."	". . . except admit that you're completely at fault."
"I just feel like I'm not getting anywhere in my life."	"I just feel like everyone's getting married but me."
"My friend Karen went through this too."	". . . before she got married."

DEPRESSION: MALE-TO-ENGLISH

Male . . .

"Nothing's wrong."

"It's not about you."

"There's nothing you can do."

"I just feel like I'm not getting anywhere in my life."

"My friend Stuart went through this too."

English . . .

"Something's wrong."

"It's about you."

". . . except have sex with me."

"I just feel like everyone's getting rich but me."

". . . after he got married."

RELATIONSHIP TALK: FEMALE-TO-ENGLISH

Female . . .	English . . .
"There's something I want to talk about."	"What are your intentions in this relationship?"
"Let's spend some time together."	"Let's spend several hours talking about our relationship."
"Let's spend some special time together."	"Let's have an all-day picnic in the park and hold hands and say 'I love you,' and discuss the future of this relationship."
"Let's try couples therapy."	"Let's get a mediator to convince you to make a commitment."
"I'm just not sure we're compatible."	"I'm just not sure you want to get married."
"Let's get engaged."	"Let's pick out a ring."

RELATIONSHIP TALK: MALE-TO-ENGLISH

Male . . .

"Let's not talk right now, honey."

"Let's spend some time together."

"Let's spend some special time together."

"Let's try massage therapy."

"I'm just not sure we're compatible."

"Let's get engaged."

English . . .

"I'm not in the mood to have yet another long discussion about our relationship."

"Let's watch the baseball game together."

"Let's spend some special time together naked."

"Let's spend some special time together naked."

"I'm just not sure you want to have sex with me enough."

"Let's procrastinate."

MEETING FAMILY: FEMALE-TO-ENGLISH

Female . . .

"I want you to meet my family."

"You don't have to bring flowers or anything."

"My sister Sally really liked you."

"My mom really liked you."

"My brother Keith's a little hard to get to know."

English . . .

"I want you to know this is getting serious."

"Bring flowers or something."

"She thinks you're cute, so don't flirt with her."

"My mom thinks you'll marry me."

"My brother Keith thinks you're a snake, like my other boyfriends."

MEETING FAMILY: FEMALE-TO-ENGLISH

Female . . .

"My father really liked you."

"My family never liked a guy as much as they liked you."

"I can't believe my mom showed you my baby pictures."

"My parents have a great marriage."

English . . .

"My father thinks you can support me and my children."

"My family thought all my other boyfriends were losers."

"Tell me my baby pictures are adorable."

"We could have a great marriage."

MEETING FAMILY: MALE-TO-ENGLISH

Male . . .

"Maybe we'll stop by my family's . . ."

"You don't have to bring flowers or anything."

"My dad really liked you."

"My mom really liked you."

"My whole family really liked you."

"My sister Debbie's just a little shy sometimes."

"My family never liked a girl as much as they liked you."

"I can't believe my mom showed you my baby pictures."

"My parents have a lousy marriage."

English . . .

"I want to show off how pretty you are."

"Bring flowers or something."

"My dad thinks you're really cute."

"She thinks you'll give her grandchildren."

"Now I'll never get rid of you."

"My sister Debbie thinks you're a gold digger."

"My family thought all my other girlfriends were gold diggers."

"Don't tell me my baby pictures are adorable."

"We could have a lousy marriage."

MONEY MATTERS: FEMALE-TO-ENGLISH

Female . . .	English . . .
"I can't afford to live with you if we're not married."	"I can't afford to take the chance that you won't want to get married."
"I want to have your children . . ."	". . . after you buy me a ring . . ."
"I have my own money . . ."	". . . which I'm not sharing with you unless you want to get married."
"I think you'll make a great father."	"I think you can support children."
"If it doesn't work out, you can always divorce me . . ."	". . . and then I'll take all your money."

MONEY MATTERS: MALE-TO-ENGLISH

Male . . .	English . . .
"I can't afford to live together."	"I'm afraid to live together."
"I can't afford to get married."	"I'm afraid to get married."
"I can't afford to have children."	"I'm afraid to have children."
"I know you don't love me for my money."	"I'm afraid you love me for my money."
"I'm afraid to get married."	"I'm afraid to get divorced."
"I'm afraid to get divorced."	"I'm afraid you'll take all my money."

BREAKUPS: FEMALE-TO-ENGLISH

Female . . .

"It's not you, it's me."

"I'm not trying to pressure you."

"I need to find myself."

"I want to date other people."

"How much time do you need to decide?"

"Let's keep things open."

English . . .

"It's you."

"I'm trying to pressure you."

"I need to find myself a man who can make a commitment."

"I want to date someone else and make you jealous enough to propose."

"How many more of my childbearing years do you want to waste?"

"Maybe you'll wake up and buy me a ring."

BREAKUPS: MALE-TO-ENGLISH

Male . . .

"It's not you, it's me."

"I'm not good enough for you."

"There's no one else."

"I need to clear my head."

"I want to date other people."

"Let's keep things open."

English . . .

"It's you."

"I'm not attracted enough to you."

"There's someone else."

"I need to get some head."

"I want to sleep with other people."

"Maybe we can still sleep together sometimes."

GETTING BACK TOGETHER: FEMALE-TO-ENGLISH

Female . . .

"I missed you."

"I couldn't stand the thought of being without you."

"I'll never be jealous and controlling again."

"My place was lonely without you."

"I need you."

"Things will be different."

"I'm really relieved this is resolved."

English . . .

"I couldn't find anyone better to replace you."

"I couldn't stand the thought of you finding a prettier girl."

"I'll never be jealous and controlling again this week . . ."

"My place was neat without you."

"I need you to take me out to dinner."

"Things will be different . . . for a week."

"I'm really relieved I can get out of the dating scene."

GETTING BACK TOGETHER: MALE-TO-ENGLISH

Male . . .

"I missed you."

"I couldn't stand the thought of being without you."

"I'll never flirt with other women again."

"My cat missed you."

"I need you."

"Things will be different."

"I'm really relieved this is resolved."

English . . .

"I couldn't find anyone better to replace you."

"I couldn't stand the thought of you finding a more successful guy."

"I'll never flirt with other women again this week . . ."

"I missed somebody changing the litter."

"I need you to cook for me."

"Things will be different . . . for a week."

"I'm really relieved I can get back to work."

LIVING TOGETHER: FEMALE-TO-ENGLISH

Female . . .

"Where did you get that beer bottle collection?"

"I want you to feel comfortable here."

"I'm so happy sleeping with you every night."

"Wouldn't it be nice if we could live together forever?"

"I don't need a piece of paper to justify our love to the world."

English . . .

"Where can we lose that beer bottle collection?"

"But not so comfortable that you leave your clothes all over the floor."

"I'm so happy knowing where you're sleeping every night."

"Wouldn't it be nice if we could get married?"

"I need a piece of paper to justify our love to the world."

LIVING TOGETHER: MALE-TO-ENGLISH

Male . . .	English . . .
"Where did you get that big pink vase?"	"Where can we lose that big pink vase?"
"I feel really comfortable here."	"So comfortable that I leave my clothes all over the floor."
"I'm so happy sleeping with you every night."	"I'm so happy I don't have to deal with your paranoia about where I'm sleeping every night."
"Wouldn't it be nice if we could live together forever?"	"Wouldn't it be nice if we could live together forever without getting married?"
"I don't need a piece of paper to justify our love to the world."	"I don't need a piece of paper entitling you to half of everything I own if it doesn't work out."

WEDDING DAY: FEMALE-TO-ENGLISH

Female . . .	**English . . .**
"This is one of the happiest days of my life."	"This is one of the happiest days of my life."
"I'm glad we updated the wedding vows."	"I'm glad we took out the word 'obey.' "
"Walking down the aisle, I thought—*this is so perfect!*"	"Walking down the aisle, I thought—*he could still get away.*"
"I was happy to meet your Aunt Ida and Uncle Irving."	"I was happy that your Aunt Ida and Uncle Irving live out of town."
"Your friend Sam's toast was interesting."	"Your friend Sam's toast was completely rude and inappropriate."
"I never want this day to be over."	"I never want this day to be over."

WEDDING DAY: MALE-TO-ENGLISH

Male . . .

"This is one of the happiest days of my life."

"I'm glad we updated the wedding vows."

"Walking down the aisle, I thought—*this is so perfect!*"

"It was great to meet your cousins Phil and Sarah and the kids."

"Your friend Linda's toast was interesting."

"I never want this day to be over."

English . . .

"This is one of the scariest days of my life."

"What's wrong with 'obey?' "

"Walking down the aisle, I thought—*I can still get away.*"

"It was great to know your cousins Phil and Sarah and the kids live out of town."

"Your friend Linda's toast was ridiculously sentimental."

"I can't wait for this day to be over."

POST-MARRIED LIFE—TWO WEEKS LATER: FEMALE-TO-ENGLISH

Female . . .	English . . .
"This is one of the happiest days of my life."	"This is one of the scariest days of my life."
"I love staying home with you."	"Aren't we ever going out again?"
"I love cooking for you."	"When are you taking me out to dinner?"
"I love watching movies on the VCR with you."	"When are you taking me out to a movie?"
"I love living here with you."	"I hate cleaning up after you."
"Your socks are in the closet, dear."	". . . where you left them."
"Your shirt is in the closet, dear."	"Do you think a uterus comes with a tracking device?"

POST-MARRIED LIFE—TWO WEEKS LATER: MALE-TO-ENGLISH

Male . . .	English . . .
"This is one of the happiest days of my life."	"This is one of the happiest days of my life."
"I love staying home with you."	"I love not having to bother going out."
"I love when you cook for me."	"I love not having to take you to dinner."
"I love watching movies on the VCR with you."	"I love not having to go out to the movies."
"I love living here with you."	"I hate you rearranging all my stuff."
"Do you know where my socks are, dear?"	"Where did you put my socks, dear?"
"Do you know where my shirt is, dear?"	"Where the hell did you put my shirt?"

PREGNANCY—GETTING THE NEWS: FEMALE-TO-ENGLISH

Female . . .	English . . .
"This is one of the happiest days of my life."	"This is one of the happiest days of my life."
"I just want a healthy child."	"I just want a healthy child."
"Should we redecorate?"	"How should we redecorate?"
"I'd like a little snack."	"I'd like a little hamburger, french fries, chocolate milk shake, turkey sandwich, and pickles."
"I have a little morning sickness."	"I feel like throwing up every five minutes."
"I hope this won't change anything."	"I hope you can handle me looking like a hippopotamus."

PREGNANCY—GETTING THE NEWS: MALE-TO-ENGLISH

Male . . .

"This is one of the happiest days of my life."

"I just want a healthy child."

"How should we redecorate?"

"Do you want another little snack, dear?"

"You're just a little emotional right now, dear."

"You look beautiful."

English . . .

"This is one of the scariest days of my life."

"I just want a healthy son."

"How am I going to pay for this?"

"How am I going to pay for all the food you're shoving into your mouth?"

"You're an emotional maniac with the appetite of a hippopotamus."

"You look like a beautiful hippopotamus."

PREGNANCY—NINE MONTHS LATER: FEMALE-TO-ENGLISH

Female . . .

"This is one of the happiest days of my life."

"That wasn't so bad."

"I'm so glad you were there with me."

"He looks just like your side of the family."

"Let's never go through that again."

"I just need sleep."

English . . .

"This is one of the scariest days of my life."

"That was the worst experience I've ever had in my life."

"I'm so glad you didn't faint."

"He looks just like my side of the family."

"Let's never go through that again."

"I just need full-time help."

PREGNANCY—NINE MONTHS LATER: MALE-TO-ENGLISH

Male . . .

"This is one of the happiest days of my life."

"I'm so glad I was right there with you."

"He looks just like your side of the family."

"I can't wait to bring him home."

"Let's never go through that again."

"I just need sleep."

English . . .

"This is one of the happiest days of my life."

"I'm so glad I didn't faint."

"He looks just like my side of the family."

"I hope the bill collectors can wait."

"Let's go through that again next year."

"I just need sex."

DIVORCE: FEMALE-TO-ENGLISH

Female . . .

"I just think we should be amiable about this."

"Our prenuptial agreement is ridiculous."

"How would you like to divide up our property?"

"How would you like to divide up our assets?"

"Talk to my lawyer about it."

English . . .

"Give me more money and we'll be amiable about this."

"Our prenuptial agreement doesn't give me enough money."

"I get the house."

"I get the car, money, and kids."

"My lawyer will get me more money."

DIVORCE: MALE-TO-ENGLISH

Male . . .	English . . .
"I just think we should be amiable about this."	"If you stop asking for such a ridiculous amount of money, we can be amiable."
"Our prenuptial agreement was appropriate."	"Our prenuptial agreement doesn't give you much money."
"How would you like to divide up our property?"	"Let's sell the house and split it."
"How would you like to divide up our assets?"	"You can have half the house, the car, and the kids. Just get me out of here."
"Can we leave the lawyers out of it?"	"My lawyer is ripping me off almost as much as you are."

CONVERSION CHART: TIME

The pace of life you'll encounter on your travels might require minor adjustments to help avoid sudden jolts and jet lag. Here's a handy transformation table:

Female	Male
FIRST LOVE:	
Age 14	Age 19
FIRST MARRIAGE PANG:	
Age 19	Age 39 ½
DECIDING IF PARTNER SHOULD BECOME SPOUSE:	
Dating, 2 months	Living together, two years
DECIDING WHETHER TO HAVE CHILDREN:	
Until age 44 ½	Until age 107
TO ORGASM:	
Two hours	Two minutes

CONVERSION CHART: TIME

Female	**Male**

GETTING READY IN MORNING:

Dressing, grooming, cleaning = 1 hour, 32 minutes

Showering, shaving, dressing = 12 minutes, 14 seconds

RESTROOM DELAY:

36 women on line = 22-minute wait

94 men on line = 4-minute wait

SHOPPING:

Try on 36 garments at 7 department stores and 4 boutiques / Looking in mirror / Taking long lunch / Trying on favorites again / Purchase only a belt = 4 hours, 39 minutes

Purchase 6 identical shirts, 7 pairs of socks at first store = 12 minutes, 16 seconds

HAIR CARE:

Beauty shop for henna, cut, curl, perm, blow-dry, pedicure, manicure, makeover, leg and lip wax = $194, 3 ½ hours

Barbershop for trim = $14, 12 minutes

PHONE CONVERSATION WITH BEST FRIEND:

Comforting Lisa over latest breakup / Comparing breakup stories / Offering general relationship advice / Analyzing each other's dreams, with 3 call waitings = 2 hours, 22 minutes

Help Dave fix computer over phone = 12 minutes

CONVERSION CHART: CULTURAL REACTIONS

Differences in knowledge, belief, and behavior can lead to bad manners and utter bafflement. Become familiar with native styles, structures, and sentiments.

Female	Male
TO STRESS:	
Talking about it / Hugging	Reading the newspaper / Watching the ball game
TO A PROBLEM:	
Talking about it / Hugging	Fixing it
TO CRITICISM:	
Talking about it / Hugging	Reading the newspaper / Watching the ball game
TO INTIMACY:	
More intimacy	Reading the newspaper / Watching the ball game

CONVERSION CHART: OVERREACTIONS

Female   **Male**

"GAINING SEVEN POUNDS" MEANS:

Unfeminine, unlovable,   Gaining seven pounds
lonely, depressed,
unmarriageable, a complete
failure, an outcast, ugly,
weird, incompetent, ruined
for life . . .

"GETTING FIRED" MEANS:

Getting fired   Unmasculine, unlovable,
                                    lonely, depressed,
                                    unmarriageable, a complete
                                    failure, an outcast, ugly,
                                    weird, incompetent, ruined
                                    for life . . .

CONVERSION CHART: BAD HABITS

Female	Male
SMOKING:	
Virginia Slim Menthol Lights	Pipes / Cigars / Chewing tobacco
ALCOHOL:	
Rum and Tab / White wine spritzer	Beer / Straight bourbon
DRUGS:	
Speed / Valium / Prozac	Steroids / Angel dust / Whippets
SEX:	
Sleeping with old boyfriend	Sleeping with any girl who'll say yes
DEALING WITH CONFLICTS:	
Screaming / Swearing	Giving the finger / Mooning

CONVERSION CHART: SYMBOLS

Female	**Male**
OF AFFECTION:	
Love	Sex
OF SECURITY:	
White picket fence	Gold Mastercard
OF DOMESTICITY:	
Three kids	Three cars
OF SUCCESS:	
Six-bedroom house	Six-digit salary
OF STRENGTH:	
Psychological clarity	Physical stamina
OF METAPHYSICS:	
Astrological sign	Dollar sign

CONVERSION CHART: ESSENTIALS

Female	Male
HIDING HEIGHT PROBLEMS:	
High heels / Good posture	Cowboy boots / Elevator shoes
HIDING WEIGHT PROBLEMS:	
Wearing all black clothes	Wearing extra-large clothes
HIDING HAIR PROBLEMS:	
Wigs	Combing strands over bald spot
HIDING WRINKLES:	
Makeup	Mirrored shades

CONVERSION CHART: ESSENTIALS

Female	**Male**
EMERGENCY PHONE NUMBERS:	
Shrink / Gynecologist / Three close girlfriends / Mother / Pharmacist / Hair stylist / Personal trainer	Old girlfriend who'll still have sex / Bank access code
ACTIVITIES:	
Therapy / Shopping / Dieting	Drinking beer / Sex / Ball game
QUALITIES IN MATE:	
Good personality / Handsome face / Intelligence / Integrity / Great sense of humor / Honesty / Generosity / Ability to make commitment	Good body / Likes sex
ABBREVIATIONS:	
ERA / NOW / PMS	RBI / NBA / IRS

CONVERSION CHART: ESSENTIALS

Female	Male
UNDERGARMENTS:	
26 Pairs of lacy underwear / 17 Bras / 7 Teddies / 6 Half-slips / 3 Full slips / 9 Pairs control-top pantyhose	3 boxer shorts / White T-shirt
SHOES:	
New black pumps	Old white sneakers
ELECTIVE SURGERY:	
Breast implants	Hair implants
OVERIDENTIFICATION:	
Favorite soap-opera characters	Favorite hometown sports teams

CONVERSION CHART: ESSENTIALS

Female	**Male**
FURNITURE:	
Throw pillows / Telephone / Closet space / Drawer space / Clean sheets / New towels / End tables / Flowers in vases	TV / VCR / Stereo
DRINK:	
Diet soda	Beer
MAGAZINE:	
Cosmopolitan	*Penthouse*
REFERENCE BOOKS:	
Smart Women, Foolish Choices / *Linda Goodman's Love Signs*	*NBA Basketball Stats* / *The World's Best Dirty Jokes*
MONEY HOLDER:	
Purse containing: hairbrush, lipstick, credit cards, photographs, keys, pens, matches, Band-Aids, perfume, tissues, cash, extra pantyhose, tampons, lotion, aspirin, blush, eyeliner, eyelash curler, lighter, foundation	Wallet containing: credit card, cash, condom

CONVERSION CHART: GREETINGS

Female	Male
TO ACQUAINTANCE:	
Air kiss	Handshake
TO FRIEND:	
Hug	Pat on back
TO CLOSE FRIEND:	
Kiss	High five
TO BEST FRIEND:	
Hug and kiss	Punch on arm

CONVERSION CHART: PREPARATION

When dealing with foreign people, be prepared for different patterns and paces.

Female	Male
PARTY:	
Shop for crudités, red and white wine, soda, mixers, liquor, gourmet cheese / Polish wine glasses / Clean apartment / Buy fresh flowers / Try on everything in closet / Shop for new outfit / Buy film for camera, ice, napkins / Phone twenty friends to make sure they're coming	Buy potato chips, Doritos, plastic cups / Order keg
DATE:	
Work out for an hour in morning / Get hair cut / Clean apartment / Hide ex's photo / Try on everything in closet / Shop for new outfit / Go to shrink appointment and discuss expectations for date / Put on makeup / Blow hair dry / Spray perfume	Get dressed / Go to bank

CONVERSION CHART: PREPARATION

Female	Male
SEX:	
Work out three hours in morning / Shave legs / Apply mustache wax / Get manicure, pedicure / Use body lotion, douche, bidet, shampoo, conditioner / Take bubble bath / Curl hair / Curl eyelashes / Fix lighting / Buy wine / Clean apartment / Wash sheets / Pose in front of mirror wearing lingerie / Change clothes six times	Shower / Shave / Buy condoms

CONVERSION CHART: PREPARATION

Female	**Male**
LIVING TOGETHER:	
Throw out old scrapbooks and stuffed animals / Hide old love letters / Buy new clothes, nightgowns, towels and toiletries / Go to shrink appointment / Discuss decision with four girlfriends	Empty two drawers
MARRIAGE:	
Go to six shrink appointments / Buy new clothes / Write twenty-six pages in diary about the meaning of love and commitment in the world / Discuss in-depth with three girlfriends / Write good-bye letters to ex	Buy ring

CONVERSION CHART: PREPARATION

Female	Male
WEDDING:	
Write guest list / Pick out perfect invitations / Contact bridesmaids / Rent hall with mother / Call mother-in-law's florist / Hire caterer, photographer, bartender / Audition bands / Go on diet / Set up appointment with hairstylist, masseuse / Schedule dress fittings / Make seating arrangements / Choose silverware, menu, room colors, floral themes / Register / Invite ex and shrink	Shave / Show up

CONVERSION CHART: APARTMENT DECOR

Female	Male
ARTWORK:	
Georgia O'Keeffe print	Pamela Lee calendar
END TABLE:	
Glass / Marble	Milk crates / Brick
ANTIQUES:	
Perfume bottle collection	Beer bottle collection
BOOKSHELVES:	
Pine / Oak / Art Deco	Milk crates / Brick
DRESSER ADORNMENT:	
Pictures in silver frames / Crystal vases with fresh flowers / White candles in pewter candlestick holders	Basketball / High school bowling trophy / Bong

CONVERSION CHART: BATHROOM

Female	Male
SIGN OF ENTRY:	
Pantyhose hanging on shower	Toilet seat up
MEDICINE CHEST:	
Midol	Minoxidil
STRANGE EQUIPMENT:	
Bidet	Urinal
ANNOYING HABIT:	
Using his razor	Peeing in shower
BIRTH CONTROL:	
The pill / Morning-after pill / Diaphragm / Spermicidal jelly / I.U.D. / Sponge	Condom / Cold shower

CONVERSION CHART: ILLNESS

Female	Male
VISITS DOCTOR:	
Twice a year for checkups	When in unbearable pain
VISITS DENTIST:	
Twice a year for checkups / X-rays	When wisdom teeth get abscessed
VISITS SHRINK:	
Twice a week for seven years	When girlfriend leaves
REACTION TO MILD BACKACHE:	
Acupuncture, massage, yoga therapy / Advil / Lies flat for three days	Ignores until it gets worse
REACTION TO SEVERE BACKACHE:	
Sees doctor	Complains, groans / Has to be taken to doctor

CONVERSION CHART: CHILDHOOD

Female	Male

FAVORITE TOYS:

Female	Male
Barbie dolls / Dawn dolls / Chatty Cathy dolls / Susie Homemaker oven / Cabbage Patch dolls	BB gun / Legos / Train set / Water pistol / Plastic green army men / Dart gun / Slingshot / Ant farms / Plastic rifle / Firecrackers

FAVORITE GAMES:

Female	Male
Jump rope / Hopscotch / Jacks / Pick-up sticks / Mother-May-I? / Simon Says / Playing house	War / Tag / Tackle Football / Army / Submarine / Stratego / Risk / One-on-one

FAVORITE HOBBIES:

Female	Male
Weaving pot holders / Stringing beads / Sewing clothes for dolls / Lanyard	Canoeing through mud / Picking up stray dogs / Feeding insects to frogs / Cutting legs off grasshoppers / Sniffing airplane glue

FAVORITE ROLE PLAY:

Female	Male
Cinderella	Rambo

CONVERSION CHART: CHILDHOOD

Female	Male

FAVORITE COLORS:
Pink / Lime green

Black and blue

FAVORITE PETS:
Cats / Fish / Two little turtles
in plastic bowl with palm tree

Snakes / Rats / Tarantulas

ROLE MODELS:
Barbie / Marcia Brady / Mary
Tyler Moore / Farrah Fawcett

Superman / Hulk / Elvis /
Mickey Mantle / Muhammad
Ali / Batman / Spider-Man /
Tony Marino

RELICS:
Scrapbooks / Photo albums /
Doll collection / Bead
collection / Stuffed animals /
Dried flowers / Pot holder
collection

Baseball cards / Old teeth

CONVERSION CHART: IDEAL

Female	Male
PARTY:	
Made three business contacts / Took phone numbers of four potential new girlfriends and one potential fix-up / Heard great gossip about mutual enemy / Bumped into his old girlfriend, who'd gained twenty-two pounds	Good beer / Good music / Got cute girl's phone number
DATE:	
Ends up in love	Ends up in bed
FOREPLAY:	
One hour backrub / Half-hour foot massage / Reading poetry aloud / Half-hour of intimate conversation about past pain and where relationship is going	Taking off clothes
JOB:	
No stress	No boss
SEXUAL FANTASY:	
Walking down the aisle	Going to an orgy
RELATIONSHIP:	
No commitment problem	No commitment

CONVERSION CHART: FITNESS

Female	Male
WORK-OUT CLOTHES:	
Purple Lycra leotard / Turquoise midriff / Leg warmers / Matching socks / Water bottle filled with Evian / Sweatband / Wristband / Black gym bag / Waterproof Sports Walkman and tapes / Change belt / New cross-training high-tops	Sweats / T-shirt / Old sneakers
EXERCISE ROUTINES:	
Three sets of fifteen repetitions of three-pound hand weights, four times a week for three months	Skips workout for four months, then lifts 200-pound weights for five hours, grunting, sweating, and pulling muscle
TWO WEEK DIET:	
Eats 872 calories of low-fat food a day / Takes high-impact aerobic classes two hours a day, five times a week	Gives up beer
RESULT OF TWO-WEEK DIET:	
Loss of 1 pound, 3 ounces	Loss of 8 1/2 pounds
DISTORTED IMAGE IN MIRROR:	
Roseanne	Arnold Schwarzenegger

CONVERSION CHART: FOOD

Female	Male
BREAKFAST:	
Grapefruit and rye toast	Denny's Special: Eggs, bacon, sausage, toast, and home fries
LUNCH:	
Salad bar and banana	Pizza, hotdogs, or meatball sub, and french fries
AFTERNOON SNACK:	
Frozen yogurt	Pretzels, taco
DINNER:	
Broiled fish, broccoli, and baked potato	Red meat, french fries, and onion rings
NIGHT SNACK:	
Air-popped popcorn	Frozen pizza, beer, potato chips, and Ben & Jerry's ice cream

CONVERSION CHART: FOOD

Female	Male
IN REFRIGERATOR:	
Six apples / Six-pack of diet soda / Cottage cheese / Yogurt / Evian	Six six-packs of Bud / Leftover Chinese food with fungus growing on it / Cold pizza / Jalapeño peppers / Mustard / Kodak film
IN FREEZER:	
Frozen vanilla yogurt / Frozen Weight Watchers vegetable lasagna	Ben & Jerry's Chocolate Mocha Chip / Ben & Jerry's Chocolate Rainbow Swirl / Frozen Little Caesar's pizza / Frozen bagels / Bottle of vodka / Ben & Jerry's Rainforest Crunch / Beer mug
IN CABINET:	
Rice cakes / Popcorn / Diet corn oil / Fat-free crackers	Beer / Pretzels / Potato chips / Nacho chips / Corn chips / Stale cookies / Batteries

CONVERSION CHART: TELEPHONE MACHINES

Female	**Male**

OUTGOING MESSAGE:

| "Hi, this is Gina. How are you? I'm so sorry I'm not in to take your call but your message is very important to me, and if you leave your name, number and the time of your call, I'll be sure to get back to you as soon as possible. Thanks for calling and have a great day." | "It's Sam. Speak." |

INCOMING MESSAGE:

| "Hi, Gina. It's Lisa. How are you? I'm having a day from hell, I'm really upset. First I'm PMS-ing, then my boss yelled at me for nothing for a change and then Eric-the-jerk didn't call last night like he said he would. Can you believe it? You were right. I should have never trusted him again after the way he brought up his old girlfriend Angela in the middle of the movie two weeks ago . . ." | "Sam, it's Dave. Call me." |

CONVERSION CHART: REACTIONS TO GETTING FIRED

Female	Male

FIRST WEEK:

Female	Male
Wear all black clothes / Cry / Go to two shrink appointments / Tell everyone you know / Go shopping with Mom / Cry	Don't tell anyone / Drink beer

SECOND WEEK:

Female	Male
Go to health club / Take yoga and stretch classes / Cry / Go on diet / Go back to office to clean out desk and steal office supplies / Shake hands with ex-boss and get a great recommendation from him / Call headhunter / See shrink / Get angry / Clean apartment	Play pool

THIRD WEEK:

Female	Male
Take high-impact aerobics at health club / Get haircut / Cry / Lose weight / Retype résumé / Send out 100 of them / Buy new Armani navy-blue suit / Meet with headhunter / Go on two job interviews	Drink beer / Sleep all day

CONVERSION CHART: REACTIONS TO GETTING FIRED

Female	Male
FOURTH WEEK:	
Ace Step, Funk, and Slide class at gym / Dry tears / Go on second and third interviews for both jobs / See shrink / Take new position paying $6,000 a year more with bigger office / Call everyone you know	Buy newspaper and find page of want ads / Drink beer / Tell best friend about "minor work problems"

CONVERSION CHART: FIGHTING

Female	Male
REASON:	
She suggests he change	He refuses to change
END GOAL:	
To be loved	To win
HIDDEN IMPLICATION:	
If she wins, she knows she'll be a threat	If he wins, he knows he'll be loved
PURPOSE OF FIGHTING:	
Expressing anger, getting what she wants	Solving problem, protecting his ego
UNDERLYING DESIRE:	
To be loved more	To be right
METHOD:	
Crying, demanding, manipulating	Denying, yelling, stewing
SECRET WEAPON:	
Withholding sex	Withholding love
REACTION TO FIGHTING:	
Goes to shrink appointment / Talks to mother and six girlfriends	Pouts / Goes drinking with the guys
RESOLUTION:	
She apologizes, offers compromise or couples therapy	He decides to change, as if it were his idea

CONVERSION CHART: REACTIONS TO BREAKUP

Female	Male
FIRST NIGHT:	
Cry / Call a girlfriend who comes over with diet soda and ice cream / Look through photo albums / Read diary entries aloud and analyze all aspects of breakup till four in the morning	Drink beer / Fall asleep in front of TV
SECOND NIGHT:	
Invite old boyfriend to dinner	Invite old girlfriend to bed
REACTION TO SECOND NIGHT:	
Can't stop talking about breakup	Can't get it up
CONSOLATION FOR SECOND NIGHT:	
Dr. Ruth	Jack Daniels

CONVERSION CHART: LONG-TERM REACTIONS TO BREAKUP

Female	Male
FIRST WEEK:	
Wear all black clothes / Cry / Go to two shrink appointments / Have coffee with girlfriends and cry / Put Billie Holiday's "Good Morning Heartache" on answering machine / Go shopping with Mom / Cry	Ignore it
SECOND WEEK:	
Go to health club / Take yoga and stretch classes / Cry / Go on diet / Make plans for a vacation / Tear up his old letters and photos / Cry / See shrink / Get angry / Call his machine and hang up / Cry / Clean apartment	Ignore it / Don't shave
THIRD WEEK:	
Take high-impact aerobics at health club / Get new job / Cry / Lose weight / Throw out his old stuff / Write sad, confessional poetry / See shrink / Cry / Agree to fix-up by girlfriend	Get hit by truck

CONVERSION CHART: LONG-TERM REACTIONS TO BREAKUP

Female	Male
FOURTH WEEK:	
Ace Step, Funk, and Slide class at gym / Lose weight / Buy new clothes / Dry tears / Buy new furniture / Say yes to dinner date with new guy / Publish sad, confessional poetry / Feel happy / Finally over him	Freak out and call her

CONVERSION CHART: DIARY ENTRY

Female

Eight-page section in flowered book that reads ". . . and then he looked me straight in the eye and said, 'You know, I really care about you more than you think,' and he gently took my hand, which was tingling in his, and I smiled at him and looked him right in the eye and said, 'Well, I really care about you quite a bit too, you know.' And then I told him I had a dream about him the other night . . .

Male

Notebook list:
Sally *
Lisa ***
Paula **

REALITY CHECK: FEMALE

You can't expect an alien culture to adhere to the standards, signs, and symbols of your social milieu. To avoid confusion, disappointment, and rage, here's a reality check to keep your dreams and delusions in line.

Expectation	Actuality
LIVING TOGETHER:	
Candle-lit dinners / Long romantic discussions about your future / Exciting vacations for two / Passionate proposal in two months	Pizza dinners in front of television set / Cleaning up after him / His guy friends stopping by every night with six-packs / Passionate procrastination after four years / Couples therapy
HIS PROPOSAL:	
He gets on his knees, says, "I can't live without you. Marry me, darling," and begs her to accept his eternal love and devotion	In middle of ball game he mumbles, "I just got a job in New Jersey. Ya comin' or not?"
FRIENDS' RESPONSE TO HIS PROPOSAL:	
"Congratulations! You've just landed the best catch in the country! You're a lucky woman. I'm jealous."	"Did he get down on his knees?"

REALITY CHECK: FEMALE

Expectation

Actuality

WEDDING BLISS:

Lovely long lunches with mother / Registering for crystal and china at Saks and Barney's / Trying on designer gowns / Looking gorgeous walking down the aisle / Opening envelopes filled with generous checks from friends and rich relatives

Fighting with mother / Fighting with his mother / Fighting with florist / Fighting with Aunt Alice who wants to bring her six kids to black-tie dinner / Fighting with seamstress when dress isn't ready / Returning thirty-four kitchen appliances

REALITY CHECK: FEMALE

Expectation	Actuality
DATING:	
Romeo & Juliet	Mork & Mindy
SEX:	
Liz & Dick	Liz & Larry
FIGHTING:	
Lucy & Desi	Edith & Archie
DREAM VACATION:	
Endless Love	*My Dinner With André*
HIS DOUBLE:	
Mel Gibson	Mel Tormé

REALITY CHECK: FEMALE

Expectation	Actuality
HONEYMOON:	
Love Boat	The Poseidon Adventure
RAISING KIDS:	
The Cosby Show	The Addams Family
HAVING A ONE-NIGHT STAND:	
The Bridges of Madison County	Looking for Mr. Goodbar
HAVING A LOVE AFFAIR:	
Dr. Zhivago	Dr. Strangelove
GROWING OLD TOGETHER:	
On Golden Pond	Postcards from the Edge

REALITY CHECK: FEMALE

Expectation	**Actuality**

HIS FAMILY:
Leave It to Beaver — *The Simpsons*

HIS OFFICE:
L.A. Law — *Taxi*

HIS BOSS:
Lou Grant — The Godfather

HIS FRIENDS:
Seinfeld — *F-Troop*

HANGING OUT WITH HIS BEST BUDDY:
Butch Cassidy and the Sundance Kid — *Beavis and Butthead*

REALITY CHECK: MALE

Expectation	Actuality
LIVING TOGETHER:	
Hot sex all the time / Cold beer in the fridge / Dinner on the stove / The smell of fresh bread baking	Fighting about money, marriage, and who does the laundry / She's got PMS and is not in the mood / She wants to be taken out to dinner / She stays on the phone for two hours complaining about you to her girlfriends / She insists on couples therapy or she's moving out
HER RESPONSE TO HIS PROPOSAL:	
"Yes! You've made me the happiest woman alive! I love you madly and can't wait to spend my life making you happy!"	"I'll need some time to think about it."
FRIENDS' RESPONSE TO HIS PROPOSAL:	
"Congratulations! You've just made the smartest decision of your life, pal, and you'll never regret it"	"Did she cry?"

REALITY CHECK: MALE

Expectation	Actuality
WEDDING BLISS:	
Pick out tuxedo from *GQ* / Buy cigars / Show up	Mediate fights with her mother, your mother, florist, Aunt Alice and her six kids, and seamstress
HER NIGHT WEAR:	
Red teddy from Victoria's Secret / Obsession perfume	Sweatpants / T-shirt / strange-smelling, unidentified skin care products on face

REALITY CHECK: MALE

Expectation	Actuality
DATING:	
Bobby & Pam	Sid & Nancy
SEX:	
Donald & Marla	Donald & Ivana
FIGHTING:	
Stanley & Stella	Stiller & Meara
DREAM VACATION:	
Casablanca	*The Out-of-Towners*
HER DOUBLE:	
Paulina	Rhoda

REALITY CHECK: MALE

Expectation	Actuality
HONEYMOON:	
I Dream of Jeannie	*The Honeymooners*
RAISING KIDS:	
Father Knows Best	*Roseanne*
HAVING A ONE-NIGHT STAND:	
Last Tango In Paris	*Fatal Attraction*
HAVING A LOVE AFFAIR:	
Same Time Next Year	*Crimes and Misdemeanors*
GROWING OLD TOGETHER:	
Tender Mercies	*Enemies, A Love Story*

About the Author and Illustrator

Susan Shapiro's work has appeared in a variety of publications, including *The New York Times*, *The Washington Post*, *The Boston Globe*, *Details*, *Variety*, *People*, *Cosmopolitan*, *Glamour*, *New Woman*, *Playgirl* and *Penthouse*. She teaches humor writing courses at New York University and The New School. While writing this book, Susan became engaged to another humor writer, Charlie Rubin. The publication date conveniently coincides with the date of her marriage.

Carol Lay's cartoon and illustration work has appeared in periodicals such as *The Wall Street Journal*, *Newsweek* and *The New Yorker*, and in several comic anthologies including *Now*, *Endsville* and *Joyride*. Her cartoon strip, "Story Minute," appears regularly in the *LA Weekly*, *The San Francisco Examiner*, *The New York Press*, *Salon* (on the Internet) and in several other weekly papers.